Getting To Know...

Nature's Children

PORCUPINES

Laima Dingwall

SCHOLASTIC INC.

New York   Toronto   London   Auckland   Sydney
Mexico City   New Delhi   Hong Kong   Buenos Aires

Facts in Brief

Classification of North American porcupines

    Class: *Mammalia* (mammals)
    Order: *Rodentia* (rodents)
    Family: *Erethizontidae* (tree-porcupine family)
    Genus: *Erethizon*
    Species: *Erethizon dorsatum* (Canada Porcupine)
              Erethizon epixanthum (Yellow-haired Porcupine)

World distribution. North American species exclusive to North America. Related species found in South America, Africa, Asia, India, and southern Europe.

Habitat. Pine and other forests; scrubland.

Distinctive physical characteristics. Ever-growing front teeth with orange-colored protective coating; body mostly covered with defensive quills underneath a layer of guard hairs.

Habits. Mostly solitary; active at night; when alarmed, bristles its quills and thrashes its tail so that quills fly out.

Diet. Twigs, branches, inner tree bark, and green vegetation— leaves, shrubs, flowers.

Published by Scholastic Inc.
90 Old Sherman Turnpike, Danbury, Connecticut 06816.

SCHOLASTIC and associated logos are trademarks of Scholastic Inc.

ISBN 0-7172-6684-2

Printed in the U.S.A.

Edited by: Elizabeth Grace Zuraw
Photo Rights: Ivy Images

Photo Editor: Nancy Norton
Cover Design: Niemand Design

Have you ever wondered . . .

Try to imagine a walking pincushion. That's how the porcupine has been described. And no wonder! The porcupine has more than 30,000 sharp *quills,* needle-like spines that cover most of the top part of its body. Each one of the quills can be a painful weapon. But quills are only one chapter in a porcupine's life story.

Some campers know another chapter. They sometimes are awakened at night by the sound of loud gnawing. When they investigate, they discover that the culprit is none other than a porcupine, munching on a picnic table, a sign-post, or even a canoe paddle!

A walking pincushion that eats tables, sign-posts, and canoe paddles? As you'll discover, the porcupine is all of these things, but it's much more than that. It is also a shy, gentle, good-natured creature that just wants to be left alone.

The scientific name for the North American porcupine is Erethizon dorsatum. *That means "irritable back." An intruder that tangles with a porcupine often gets a quill attack that's more than just irritable!*

A Fast Learner

Tree-climbing is an important lesson for a baby porcupine to learn. In a tree, porcupines find safety, food, and a comfortable place to sleep.

To teach her baby how to climb, a mother porcupine climbs up a tree first. Then she chatters for her baby to join her. She keeps calling to encourage her little one as it slowly makes its way to the top.

A baby porcupine's first climb is usually its longest. That's because it might have to dig its claws into the tree several times before it gets a good grip. But with practice, the baby will soon be climbing up and down trees as easily as its mother.

In fact, a baby porcupine learns to climb trees within a week of its birth! Let's read on to find out more about this surprisingly agile animal.

The bottom of a porcupine's feet are covered with rough knobby skin that provides extra gripping power when the animal climbs trees.

This Porky is Not a Pig

Opposite page:
The name porcupine *comes from the Latin for "pig with thorns." But this animal's sharp quills and long claws make it anything but pig-like.*

Porcupines have sometimes been nicknamed "quill pig" or "porky." But the porcupine is not a pig. Perhaps it got its name because its nose is flat and snout-like, and it makes grunting sounds, like a pig.

The porcupine is a member of the rodent family. *Rodents* are animals with a certain kind of teeth that are especially good for gnawing. The porcupine's North American cousins include the mouse, rat, woodchuck, squirrel, gopher, and beaver.

Like all rodents, the porcupine has strong front teeth that never stop growing. But the porcupine doesn't have to worry about its teeth growing so long that it will trip over them! It keeps its teeth ground down by gnawing on tree bark.

North American porcupines have quilled cousins in Africa and Asia. But they are not related to two other quilled animals—the hedgehog and the spiny anteater.

A Fat Cat with Quills?

Next to the beaver, the porcupine is the largest rodent in North America. A full-grown male porcupine weighs 11-13 pounds (5-6 kilograms)—about the same as a big fat house cat. But some well-fed male porcupines weigh in at almost twice that weight. The average male porcupine measures about 3 feet (1 meter) from the tip of its nose to the end of its tail. The female is slightly smaller.

Where porcupines live in North America

Porcupine Country

Porcupines live in most parts of North America, except the southeastern United States and northern Alaska and the Yukon. Some porcupines live in dense forests, while others live in scrubland, often along rivers.

A porcupine is about the size of a house cat, but all those quills and fur make it look more roly-poly.

11

Tree Lover

Just think how handy it would be if your bed had a built-in kitchen cupboard. You would hardly have to disturb yourself at all when you wanted a snack—you'd just roll over and reach in. Well, porcupines can do just that! For them, a tree is both a resting place and a food supply.

Fortunately, the porcupine is well equipped for climbing trees. It digs its long curved claws into the bark, pushing with its rear paws and pulling itself up with its front paws. While climbing, it uses its broad sturdy tail as a prop. How? On the underside of its tail are stiff bristly hairs that dig into the tree's bark a bit like sandpaper.

Once it's up in the tree, the porcupine sits back and munches on tasty branches, bark, and leaves, or sprawls out and snoozes.

When a porcupine climbs down a tree, it uses its tail as a feeler to tell it when it has reached the ground.

On the Ground

When a porcupine wants to return to ground level, it shimmies down the tree tailfirst.

If you see a porcupine on the ground, you'll notice that it has short stubby legs. And it is slightly bow-legged and pigeon-toed. This gives the porcupine a clown-like, waddling walk or an awkward gallumping gallop if it's in a hurry.

However agile a porcupine may be in a tree, on the ground it moves with a slow and clumsy shuffle.

The Hairy Porcupine

A porcupine has three kinds of hair. In cold weather it grows an inner layer of thick underfur to keep in body heat. Much of this underfur falls out in late spring, when the weather warms up.

To keep out rain and snow, the porcupine's coat has *guard hairs,* long shiny coarse hairs that make up the outer layer of the coat. These guard hairs, brownish-black in color, not only keep the porcupine dry, they also make good *camouflage*—they blend in with the porcupine's surroundings so that enemies don't easily notice it.

But the porcupine is best known for its third kind of hair—its quills.

Even though its quills are excellent weapons, a porcupine prefers not to fight. If threatened, it would just as soon escape up a tree.

Hair That Hurts

You might find it a surprise to learn that a porcupine's quills are made of hardened hair. The point of each quill is covered with *barbs,* or tiny projections. These barbs lie flat against the quill when it is going into an intruder's flesh. But when the quill is being pulled out, the barbs open up a bit like an umbrella, and hook into the flesh. Ouch! Removing a quill can be very painful and difficult.

Every part of the porcupine's body is covered with these yellowish-white, barbed quills, except for areas on its face, belly, and the underside of its tail. Some quills can be as much as 4 or 5 inches (10 or 13 centimeters) long; others are the length of small pins.

A porcupine's hollow, tubed-shaped, and needle-sharp quills—shown here close-up—make good weapons.

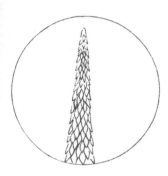

Closed barbs

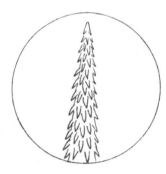

Open barbs

Stay Away—Or Else!

Most of the time you probably won't even notice a porcupine's quills. That's because they are usually covered by guard hairs as they lie flat against the porcupine's body. But once the porcupine is threatened or annoyed, muscles under its skin pull the quills so that they stand up. Then the porcupine is armed to defend itself.

Because most of the porcupine's quills are on its back and tail, it turns its back on enemies to protect itself. Then it stiffens its legs, arches its back, and lowers its head to the ground to defend its unprotected face and belly. As a last-minute warning it may chatter its teeth and hiss or even stomp its feet. Any animal that is foolhardy enough to ignore this "Stay Away" message is in for a nasty surprise.

When a porcupine loses a quill, a new one grows in to take its place. It takes between two and eight months for a new quill to grow in.

Ouch!

Some people think that a porcupine aims
and shoots its quills at enemies, but that's not
true. The quills are loosely attached to the
porcupine's skin, especially on the tail. When
the porcupine turns its back toward an enemy
and thrashes its tail back and forth to defend
itself, some of the quills fly out.

Most of these quills land on the ground and
do no harm. But if an enemy puts its nose or
mouth too close to a porcupine, it is almost
sure to leave with a faceful of quills. That's
not only painful; it can be dangerous. An
animal with quills in its mouth may not be
able to eat, and can starve to death.

With this coatful of painful weapons, it's
not surprising that the porcupine has few
enemies. But some animals, such as
wolverines, bobcats, and fishers, manage to
dodge the porcupine's quill-covered tail and
back, and flip the porcupine upside down.
That leaves the porcupine's quill-less
stomach unprotected.

A Porcupine Feast

What does a porcupine eat? Almost anything that grows! A typical porcupine menu might include leaves, flowers, and shrubs. In the summer, a porcupine will even wade belly-deep into a pond to feast on pond lilies and other water plants. If it's really hungry, it may paddle right across a pond in search of a tasty treat. Porcupines are good swimmers. Their hollow quills make a kind of natural life jacket.

But by far the porcupine's favorite foods are twigs and the inner bark of trees. North American porcupines prefer cone-bearing trees such as pines and firs. Unlike a beaver, which cuts down whole trees to get at the bark, a porcupine climbs a tree and chews on the branches. Sometimes, if a porcupine takes too big a bite, a branch will break off and fall to the ground. These "porcupine leftovers" help feed deer and rabbits in winter when other food is scarce. Porcupines eat so much bark during their lifetime that they themselves smell a bit like old wood or sawdust!

Opposite page:
A porcupine's favorite food is tree bark, but twigs and tender green plants make a fine snack, too.

Chompers To Gnaw With

If you had to bite chunks of bark off trees for your dinner, you'd need extra-strong teeth like the porcupine's. Luckily for the porcupine, its front bark-biting teeth never stop growing. Although they do get worn down from all that gnawing, more tooth grows in.

The porcupine's teeth are also very sharp. The outer part of the teeth has a tough orange-colored protective covering. As the porcupine bites off pieces of bark, the backs of the teeth wear down faster than the fronts. This helps to sharpen the tips of the teeth.

The porcupine has 16 other large flat teeth in its mouth for chewing and grinding its food.

Sturdy gnawing teeth make easy work for this porcupine when it peels the bark from an evergreen tree.

Strange Taste

Imagine how surprised some campers must be when they wake to find a porcupine munching on a pair of smelly sneakers. Eating stinky old shoes might sound pretty disgusting to you, but a porcupine finds them a delicious snack! That's because porcupines love anything that has been touched by perspiring human hands—or feet. When the perspiration dries, a trace of salt is left behind. Salt is a special treat to a porcupine.

Besides chomping on old running shoes, salt-loving porcupines have been known to eat canoe paddles, handles of tools, plywood signs, lawn furniture, and even the steering wheel of a car!

This porcupine is munching on the bark of a tree, but an even tastier treat would be a pair of old shoes.

Night Wanderers

The porcupine is a *nocturnal* animal, it is active mainly at night. That's when the porcupine wakes up and starts exploring. It waddles alone through the dark, looking for food. It may find a lush meadow where it can munch on flowers and leaves to its heart's and stomach's content, or it may spot a tasty-looking tree to gnaw. If a porcupine finds a good feeding spot it will go back night after night, following the same path it used the night before.

A favorite item in a porcupine's diet is bark. Porcupines prefer the bark of evergreen trees.

Daytime Sleepers

The porcupine snoozes for most of the day, usually up in a tree. If you look very carefully next time you take a walk in the woods, you just might see a sleeping porcupine stretched out on a branch with its legs dangling down.

But sleeping porcupines are usually difficult to spot. The porcupine's long guard hairs make it look like a clump of leaves or a bird's nest. Don't be tempted to climb up and take a closer look, though. If the porcupine is disturbed, it may back down the tree and thrash a tail full of quills against you.

You might not consider a treetop a good place for a snooze, but a porcupine considers it ideal.

A Nearsighted Sniffer

If you were nose to nose with a porcupine, you would see two dark little eyes staring back at you. And the porcupine is *nearsighted*—it could see you very well at that close range, but if you moved back several steps it might have trouble getting you into focus. However, thanks to its sensitive nose, the porcupine would still know you were there.

The porcupine relies on its keen sense of smell to help it find food. Since it searches for food at night when its eyesight is of little use, having a sharp nose makes a lot of sense. To put its super sniffer to best use, it walks with its nose to the ground or sits back on its haunches with its nose turned up to smell the air for food. When the porcupine finds something to eat, it usually gives the snack one last sniff before popping the food into its mouth.

Like a cat, a porcupine has whiskers growing out from the sides of its snout and cheeks. And much like a cat's whiskers, the porcupine's whiskers are sensitive feelers.

Love Songs and Dances

Porcupines like to live by themselves. If two porcupines meet, they usually ignore each another. The only time porcupines are seen together is in the fall, during *mating season,* the time when animals *mate,* or come together to produce young. Then the usually shy male porcupine sets out to attract a female.

If two males cross each other's path during mating season, they may stand up on their hind legs and have a pretend fight. But after a few minutes, they lose interest in the fight and go off on their own to find mates.

To attract a mate, the male wanders through the forest singing a loud love song made up of hums, whines, grunts, and chatterings. The female, who finds these songs hard to resist, usually joins in with her own whines and coos to make a porcupine duet. The porcupine pair then dances together. They stand up on their hind legs and walk toward one another, whining and humming as they go. After sniffing each other, they put their paws on each other's shoulders and rub noses.

Wintertime Porcupines

Porcupines that live in cold climates do not *hibernate,* or go into a kind of heavy sleep in the winter. They are active all winter long. They rarely have to worry about where their next meal is coming from because food is as close as the nearest tree.

If the weather turns bitterly cold, a porcupine might curl up in a *den,* an animal home, abandoned by another animal. It might even bed down in a corner of an empty barn or rock cave.

Most of the winter the porcupine just tries to ignore the cold. It climbs up a tree where it is out of the snow and has its food supply right under its nose. Porcupines often spend weeks, even months, up the same tree, and even through severe cold.

Porcupines don't hibernate, so they can be active all winter long. A porcupine sometimes digs tunnels in the snow to get around.

Presenting the Baby Porcupine

When spring comes, it's time for a mother porcupine to find a sheltered spot in some shrubs, a hollow log, or a rock den to use as a nursery. A female has one baby porcupine, called a *cub,* in spring or early summer.

A newborn porcupine weighs about 1 pound (half a kilogram) and measures about 12 inches (31 centimeters) from its nose to its tail. Its eyes are open at birth, and it has eight teeth, including tiny front gnawing teeth. Half an hour after it's born, a baby porcupine can walk on its own.

The cub is born with a thick coat of soft black hair about as long as your pinky finger. Even its quills are soft, but in just a few hours they harden into small versions of its mother's quills.

Porcupine babies are well-developed at birth. In fact, a newborn porcupine is larger than a newly born black bear, even though the adult bear is many times larger than the adult porcupine.

Porcupine Lessons

The female porcupine raises her baby alone. When it is only a couple of days old, she begins to teach it how to climb up and down trees and to find food and shelter.

When it is not practicing tree climbing or food finding, the little porcupine snoozes under logs or among brush or low shrubs. Unlike its mother, who stays up her tree until dark, the young porcupine may wander around on the ground during the day, usually because it is hungry.

Even though a baby porcupine drinks its mother's milk until it is about six or seven weeks old, it starts to munch tender blades of grass, tree seedlings, herbs, and shrubs as early as two weeks after birth.

A little nudge from its mother helps a baby porcupine learn to climb a tree.

Playful Porcupines

If two little porcupines meet, they sometimes play-fight and chase one another in fun. This play-fighting helps the cubs learn how to defend themselves.

Baby porcupines, like most young animals, seem to love play—even if they're all alone. They have been seen walking stiff-legged and spinning around quickly in a circle like prickly tops.

Born in the spring or early summer, porcupine cubs learn survival techniques quickly, and reach complete maturity by fall of the year.

On Its Own

Mother and baby porcupine stay together for only about two months. They aren't seen together often, but they are always within calling distance of one another. The mother keeps track of her baby by chattering and making other noises. She "talks" to her baby when it is time to leave its daytime sleeping spot or when she wants it to climb a tree.

By fall the young porcupine is ready to go off on its own. If it has learned its porcupine survival lessons well, it will live to be about nine years old.

Other animals will keep a safe distance and other porcupines will leave it alone, but the young porcupine will not be lonely. It will take long snoozes during the daytime and explore for food at night, quite content to be on its own.

Words To Know

Barbs   Projections at the end of a porcupine quill that help it lodge in an intruder's flesh.

Camouflage   Coloring and markings on an animal that blend in with its surroundings.

Cub   Name of the young of various animals, including the porcupine.

Den   Animal home.

Guard hairs   Long coarse hairs that make up the outer layer of a porcupine's coat.

Hibernate   To fall into a kind of heavy sleep during the winter. When animals hibernate, their breathing and heart rates slow, and their body temperature goes down.

Mate   To come together to produce young.

Mating season   The time when animals mate.

Nearsighted   To be able to see things clearly only at close range.

Nocturnal   Active mostly at night.

Quills   Needle-like spines that cover most of the top part of a porcupine's body.

Rodent   An animal with certain kind of teeth that are especially good for gnawing.

Index

PHOTO CREDITS
Cover: Bill Ivy. **Interiors:** Bill Ivy, 4, 9, 28, 31. /*Valan Photos:* Joseph R. Pearce, 7; Stephen J. Krasemann, 16, 39; Michel Bourque, 19; Dennis W. Schmidt, 37. /*Ivy Images:* Lynn & Donna Rogers, 10, 25, 35, 42. /Barry Ranford, 13. /Tom W. Parkin, 15. /Leonard Lee Rue III, 21. /*Visuals Unlimited:* D. Cavagnaro, 22. /Thomas Kitchin, 27, 44. /Duane Sept, 33. /Vince Claerhout, 40.

Getting To Know...

Nature's Children

GRIZZLY BEARS

Caroline Greenland

SCHOLASTIC INC.

New York Toronto London Auckland Sydney
Mexico City New Delhi Hong Kong Buenos Aires

Facts in Brief

Classification of the Grizzly Bear

Class: *Mammalia* (mammals)
Order: *Carnivora* (meat-eaters)
Family: *Ursidae* (bear family)
Genus: *Urus*
Species: *Ursus arctos* (Brown Bear)
Subspecies: *Ursus arctos horribilis* (Grizzly Bear)

World distribution. Exclusive to North America; closely related to the European Brown Bear, which lives in Europe and Asia.

Habitat. Seem to prefer open meadows and river valleys but may also be found in forests and lower mountain slopes.

Distinctive physical characteristics. Very large; thick, gray-flecked fur, especially long around neck; long, curved claws.

Habits. Solitary; usually establishes territory, marking it by clawing trees; winters in den but is not a true hibernator.

Diet. Will eat whatever is available—roots, leafy plants, berries, small animals, fish.

Published by Scholastic Inc.
90 Old Sherman Turnpike, Danbury, Connecticut 06816.

SCHOLASTIC and associated logos are trademarks of Scholastic Inc.

ISBN 0-7172-6684-2   Printed in the U.S.A.

Edited by: Elizabeth Grace Zuraw   *Photo Editor:* Nancy Norton
Photo Rights: Ivy Images   *Cover Design*: Niemand Design

Have you ever wondered . . .

How did the Grizzly Bear get its name? It may be because of the color of its coat. The tips of the fur are *grizzled,* or flecked with gray. Or it may be because the Grizzly Bear is thought to be fierce. Something that is terrible or frightening is often described as *grisly.*

Whatever the origin of its name, the Grizzly does have a bad reputation. Even though Grizzlies are intelligent and shy, many people think of them as ferocious and dangerous. Usually, the only Grizzlies that will attack a person are a mother bear protecting her cubs or a Grizzly that is cornered or startled.

In those rare cases where a Grizzly does attack, it will fight with courage and great strength. But most of the time Grizzlies don't look for trouble.

Grizzlies can look as fuzzy and cuddly as a teddy bear, but this is one bear you don't want to hug.

Meet a Grizzly Bear Cub

Fishing can be pretty hard work for a Grizzly Bear cub. There are so many delicious salmon swimming along—and they're just out of reach. But maybe if the cub stretches its paw out just a little more…and then leans over just a little bit and…SPLASH!

But you needn't worry. All Grizzly cubs know how to swim. Besides, if this cub doesn't manage to catch a fish soon, its mother will catch one for her little one. Like all Grizzly babies, this cub will sit nervously on the riverbank, straining to keep its mother in sight while she fishes. But as soon as she returns with a fish, the cub will be happy and playful again, knowing its protector is close by.

If you would like to know more about this appealing little creature—and big Grizzly Bears, too—read on.

Grizzly cubs quickly learn not to disobey their mother. That's because she not only will scold them but will probably cuff them with her paw.

The Bear Facts

The Grizzly Bear is one of the largest animals in North America. Male Grizzlies, called *boars,* are usually larger than females, or *sows.* Most boars weigh about 700 pounds (320 kilograms). Some may weigh as much as seven grown men! Male Grizzlies keep on growing throughout their lives, so the older they get, the bigger they are.

Grizzlies often look bigger than they really are because of their long, thick fur. The hair around a Grizzly's neck is especially long. It looks like a ruff or cape and flops around as the bear runs.

Grizzly Bears may be any color, from creamy yellow to nearly black. But no matter what the color, the fur is flecked with gray, giving it the grizzled look.

Bears growl, whine, cry, and bawl. And when they're surprised, they say something that sounds like "whooosh."

Bear Country

There are bears in many countries, but you'll find the Grizzly Bear only in North America. Some Grizzlies live in Mexico, but most are in the northwestern United States, western Canada, and Alaska.

Grizzly Bears seem to prefer living in open meadows or river valleys. But they also live in forests at the bottom of mountains. Some may even wander into the treeless wilderness areas of the North.

Where Grizzly Bears live in North America

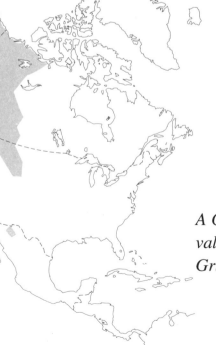

A Grizzly looks out over a deep river valley, one of the types of places that Grizzlies prefer to live in.

Bear Relatives

Grizzlies are related to Polar Bears and Black Bears. Their closest cousins, however, are the Alaskan Brown Bear and the European Brown Bear, which lives in Europe and Asia.

Black Bear

All of these bears have certain things in common. They eat meat as well as plants, and they have two kinds of teeth to chew food. They walk flat on their feet, and their front feet are slightly pigeon-toed. This makes a bear look clumsy and slow when it walks.

Grizzly Bear

Polar Bear

Grizzlies belong to a group of bears called Big Brown Bears. Alaskan Brown Bears, such as the one shown here, look a lot like the Grizzly but are even bigger. All Brown Bears have a hump on the shoulders, just behind the neck—a quick and easy way to identify them.

Stay Out

Most Grizzly Bears have their own *territory,* an area where an animal lives and spends most of its time. For a Grizzly, this piece of land may be as large as 6 square miles (16 square kilometers). If food is scarce, the Grizzly's territory may be even bigger.

To let other bears know that a territory is already taken, a Grizzly leaves long claw marks on trees as high up as it can reach. Any bear who ignores these "stay out" signs may be in for a fight.

Grizzly Bears can grow to a height of 8 feet (2.4 meters). They stand up to check out their surroundings and to scare enemies away. Native Americans called Grizzlies "the beasts that walk like people." Looking at this picture, it's easy to see why.

Super Sniffer and Sharp Ears

Look at the Grizzly Bear's long snout. Do you think that it has a keen sense of smell? If you said "yes," you're right. The Grizzly uses its sensitive nose to search for food and to avoid other animals. It needs such a good nose for many reasons. For one thing, it can't see very well. For another, the Grizzly is most active from dusk to dawn, when eyesight is not all that useful.

Like most animals that are *nocturnal,* or active in the dark, the Grizzly has excellent hearing in addition to a good sense of smell. Those furry, rounded ears can even pick up the sound of a twig cracking far away.

Grizzlies have a keen sense of smell and can sniff out dinner from a long way off.

On the Move

You may think that a Grizzly Bear looks pretty clumsy as it lumbers along. And with its big shoulders hunched over and its head held low and swinging back and forth, it may look slow, too. But for short distances, a Grizzly Bear can run about as fast as a horse.

The Grizzly walks and runs on its whole foot just as people do. Many other animals, such as horses, deer, and dogs, walk on their toes. Being flat-footed means the Grizzly can stand upright and even take a few steps on its hind legs. This is useful when its curiosity is aroused. By standing as tall as possible, it can pick up interesting smells with its super nose.

Grizzly Bear tracks

Grizzlies are powerful, fearless, aggressive, and unpredictable—good reasons for people and other animals to avoid them.

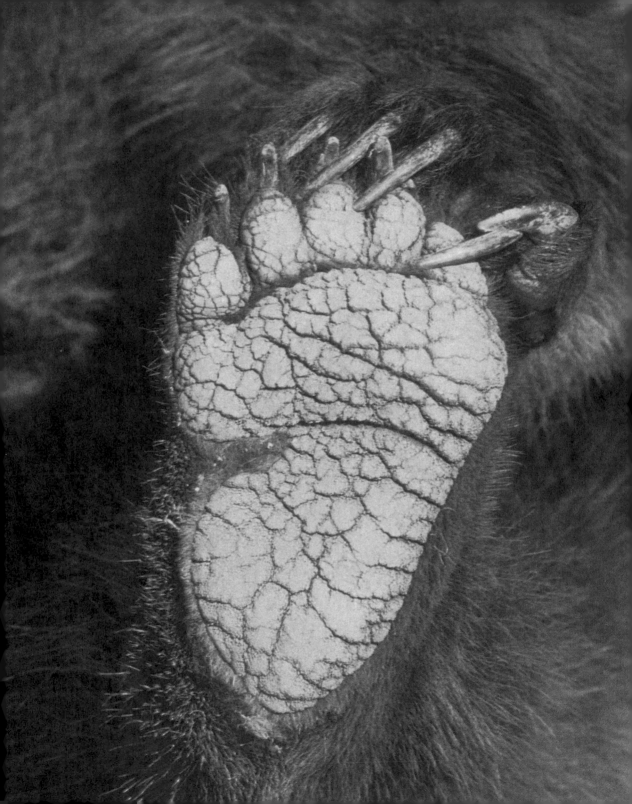

Bear Feet

A Grizzly Bear has five toes on each foot, and every toe has a long curved claw that is about the length of a new crayon. These claws help the bear dig roots and catch fish. After a summer of digging, the bear's claws get worn down. But they grow back over the winter to full length, ready for a new season of digging.

You can tell how old a Grizzly is just by looking at its claws. A young Grizzly's claws are usually black or very dark brown with light tips. But as the bear grows older, its claws get lighter in color. Some very old bears have pure white claws.

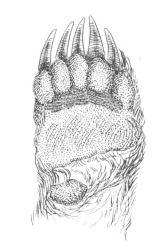

Grizzly's front foot

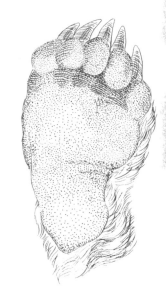

Grizzly's back foot

A bear's long, curved claws can always be seen because, unlike those of a cat, they have no covering and can't be drawn in.

What an Appetite!

In the wild, Grizzlies eat just about anything that's available—young plants, roots, grasses, berries, insects, and fish. The Grizzly eats any meat that it finds, too. Sometimes it goes after *prey,* animals hunted by other animals for food.

A Grizzly uses its long claws to dig out mice, Ground Squirrels, and marmots from their underground homes. It also hunts elk, moose, and Mountain Sheep.

If a Grizzly has more meat than it can eat at one sitting, it drags off the leftovers and hides them from other hungry animals by covering them with branches. In this way, the Grizzly can have meal after meal by returning to the hiding place.

Grizzlies usually sleep during the day and feed in the evening and at night. But if food is scarce, a Grizzly may hunt for food during the day, too.

A Bad Habit

Have you ever visited the local dump while you were out camping or at a cottage? You probably weren't the only visitor. Many bears, including Grizzlies, feast on food left behind by people.

Food that it finds in the wild is much better for a Grizzly than leftover human food. Our leftovers contain too much sugar. If a Grizzly eats too much of it, it might get cavities. And there is nothing more miserable than a bear with a sore tooth.

Overleaf:
Grizzlies most often are loners, but will gather in large numbers at a good feeding spot. A river flowing with salmon is sure to attract many Grizzlies.

Grizzlies often rummage around campsites and dumps in search of leftover human food.

Expert Fishers

In the summer, Grizzlies on the west coast crowd along riverbanks to feast on their favorite food, salmon. As the salmon swim upriver to lay their eggs, the bears prepare for a feast. The strongest bears make sure they get the best fishing spots, and they defend these places with growls and threatening head swings if another bear comes too near. The youngest bears have to make do with the spots that are left over.

A Grizzly has two ways of catching fish. It can stand in the water and swiftly scoop out a salmon with its paw. This fish dinner is then carried to the side of the river and eaten whole. Or the bear can stay on the riverbank watching carefully. The instant a salmon happens to swim by—SPLASH!—in goes the hungry Grizzly after it.

Most Grizzlies can catch between two and four fish per hour.

Open Wide!

Because of its varied diet, a Grizzly bear needs teeth that can chew a lot of different foods. Grizzly *molars,* the flat teeth at the back of the mouth, are good for grinding plant stems and roots. A Grizzly's front teeth are large and pointed. They're good for tearing into prey.

A Grizzly has 42 teeth, including the powerful *canines,* the long, pointed, front teeth on each side of the jaw. Old bears have especially long canines because bear teeth continue to grow throughout the animal's life.

Grizzlies are omnivores, *they eat both meat and plants. This bear's awesome teeth can easily handle all kinds of food.*

Mating Season

A Grizzly Bear rarely has anything to do with another Grizzly—except during *mating season,* the time of year during which animals come together to produce young. A female mates with a male every other year in June and July. Then the two Grizzlies go their separate ways. When the cubs are born the next winter, the mother Grizzly raises them on her own.

Usually unfriendly with one another, Grizzlies stay together during mating season. A male and female become quite playful, rubbing noses when they're ready to mate. They may also give each other a gentle bear hug.

Cold Weather Signals

If you were to observe a Grizzly Bear closely, you'd be able to tell when the cold weather was about to arrive. First you would look at the Grizzly's fur. As the days get colder, the Grizzly grows an extra-thick fur coat. This coat is actually two coats in one. The inner coat, the thick short *underfur,* traps body-warmed air next to the Grizzly's skin. The outer coat, made of long *guard hairs,* helps shed rain or snow that might chill the bear.

Next you would watch how much the Grizzly eats. In the fall, it eats as much food as it can find. The bear isn't unusually hungry; it's just trying to put on weight. The fatter the bear is, the better its chance of surviving a long cold winter with little or no food.

And you will know for sure that winter is very near when the Grizzly starts searching for a *den,* a shelter used as a home by an animal.

In the fall, in order to get fattened up enough to survive the cold winter ahead, a Grizzly may eat 80 to 90 pounds (36 to 40.5 kilograms) of food a day.

Digging in

By mid-November food becomes scarce, so the Grizzly starts to search for a place to sleep away the winter. Caves, hollow logs, or shelters under fallen trees make the best dens.

If a Grizzly can't find a den, it must make one for itself. It uses its long claws to dig a hole, often under a rock on a steep hill. When the Grizzly has dug a bear-size hole, it lines the den with dead leaves, branches, and grass. Then it climbs in and waits for snow to cover the den entrance. The snow helps to keep the bear's den hidden from other animals until spring.

It may be cold outside, but a Grizzly is cozy when it tucks itself into its den. A hole dug in a hillside makes a comfortable winter home.

A Long Sleep

During the winter, some animals *hibernate,* they go into a kind of heavy sleep in which their breathing and heart rate slow, and their body temperature drops. Although the Grizzly sleeps away most of the winter, its long sleep isn't true hibernation. The bear's breathing rate and body temperature change very little, and it may occasionally wake up during the winter. It may even move around outside the den if the weather is mild. True hibernators, such as Ground Squirrels, do not wake up at all until spring arrives. But whether it's true hibernation or not, Grizzlies spend the winter months in their snug dens.

A Grizzly occasionally leaves its den during the winter, especially if the weather turns mild.

Baby Bears

Opposite page: *A Grizzly mother and cub stay together for one or two years.*

Many animal babies are born in the spring, but not Grizzly cubs. They're born in mid-winter. One of the first sounds the newborns hear is the winter wind howling outside the den. But the kitten-size Grizzly cubs don't have to worry about getting cold. They snuggle up close to their mother's warm, furry body to stay warm.

As the winter winds blow and the snow flies, the cubs *nurse,* drink milk from their mother's body. Usually two cubs are born at the same time, but the number can vary from one to four. The cubs weigh at most one pound (about half a kilogram) at birth, and their eyes don't open until they're about a month old. But doing nothing besides sleeping and drinking their mother's rich milk, the cubs grow quickly. In about two months, they weigh around 20 pounds (9 kilograms). By then the den is getting crowded—and it's spring, time for the bear family to go outside.

Bear School

When spring arrives, the Grizzly cubs come rolling out of their den looking like fat, furry balls. They're frisky and ready to play—but their mother has other ideas. It's time for bear school. The cubs have to learn the lessons they need in order to survive.

The young bears stay with their mother for one or two years. By watching her, the cubs learn how to hunt and how to tell which foods are good to eat and which ones must be avoided. And they learn which animals are dangerous to young cubs.

Adult Grizzlies have few enemies. Though they're peaceful animals, when they do need to defend themselves, one blow from their powerful front paw can kill even a large enemy. But cubs are in danger from *predators,* animals that hunt other animals for food. Sometimes, even adult male Grizzlies attack Grizzly cubs.

Opposite page: *A young Grizzly cub stays close on its mother's heels even if that means wading into a stream behind her.*

A Good Mother

The Grizzly is a good mother. She protects her cubs and can be quite fierce if she thinks they are in danger. She's a good teacher, too. Most of the time she is patient and kind. But sometimes she'll cuff the cubs if they're doing something that could be dangerous.

When they first leave the den, the Grizzly cubs stay close on their mother's heels. But by the end of their first summer, their mother starts letting them go off together to explore on their own.

Grizzlies, even cubs, like to live in open areas rather than in forests.

Growing Up

During the next winter, the cubs stay with their mother and share a den with her. But come spring, the female is ready to mate again, and the youngsters are shooed away— sometimes not too gently. The sow will have plenty to do looking after her new cubs without having to worry about the two-year-olds as well.

The young bears then rely on each other to stay out of danger. The next winter they may den together, but in the spring they'll separate, each going its own way. If they remember everything their mother has taught them, they can live for as long as 25 years as magnificent Grizzlies in the wild.

Words To Know

Boar   Male bear.

Den   An animal home or shelter.

Guard hairs   Long coarse hairs that make up the outer layer of a Grizzly's coat.

Hibernation   A kind of heavy sleep that some animals take in the winter, during which their breathing and heart rates slow, and their body temperature drops.

Mate   To come together to produce young.

Mating season   The time of year when animals mate.

Molars   Back teeth that are suited for grinding food.

Nocturnal   Active mainly at night.

Nurse   To drink milk from a mother's body.

Omnivores   Animals that eat both plants and meat.

Predator   An animal that hunts other animals for food.

Prey   An animal hunted by other animals for food.

Sow   Female bear.

Territory   The area that an animal or group of animals lives in and often defends against other animals of the same kind.

Underfur   Thick short hair that traps body-warmed air next to a Grizzly's skin.

Index

PHOTO CREDITS
Cover: Bill Ivy. **Interiors:** *Valan Photos:* Stephen J. Krasemann, 4, 8, 16, 19, 23, 35, 38, 45; Brian Milne, 12, 41, 42. */Canada In Stock / Ivy Images:* Gary Crandall, 7, 28. */Tom Stack & Associates:* John Shaw, 11, 15; Thomas Kitchin, 20. /Wayne Lynch, 24. /Mark Emery, 26-27, 36. /Thomas Kitchin, 31, 32.